IMAGINARY IMAGES

IMAGINARY IMAGES

GLORIA MORRIS

JUPITER : LONDON

FIRST PUBLISHED IN 1978 BY
JUPITER BOOKS (LONDON) LIMITED
167 HERMITAGE ROAD, LONDON N4 1LZ.

ISBN 0 904041 74 3

COMPOSED IN 14PT MONOTYPE CENTAUR, SERIES 252, BY
HBM TYPESETTING LIMITED, CHORLEY, LANCASHIRE.
PRINTED AND BOUND IN GREAT BRITAIN.

CONTENTS

ACKNOWLEDGEMENTS

THE majority of the works in this volume were cast for me by the Morris Singer Foundry in England, and to them I owe a special debt of thanks. Robert Updergraff photographed all of the works and the results he obtained are quite beyond criticism. Lastly, I would like to thank my dear friend Beata de Frankovszky for patiently assisting me with the translations into French.

GLORIA MORRIS
Paris 1977

11

PREFACE

'THE PLACE AND FUNCTION of art in contemporary life' was the title of a symposium organized by UNESCO in September 1976. The purpose of this event was to define the concept of the utility and necessity of art in the different societies which man has established. A panel of distinguished artists, writers, and sociologists considered such questions as the relation of art to life-long education, the role of criticism in the development of art and in the aesthetic education of the public, art as an essential part of the human environment, art and social development, the convergence of artistic disciplines, and art and international co-operation.

Of particular relevance to the present book was the discussion on the rapidly developing convergence of artistic disciplines: the use of two- or three-dimensional objects in painting, kinetic art, music, and theatre was seen as so many examples of the recent trend which is linking up contemporary Western art with the ancient traditions of Asia and Africa, more especially in the performing arts.

In the plastic arts, such tendencies emphasize the link between the artist and the craftsman. There are already encouraging signs of the revival of certain crafts which, in industrialized countries, had been allowed to go out of existence.

Speaking at the UNESCO symposium, the eminent French sociologist Jean Duvignaud advocated the abolition of the existing hierarchy between the different forms of artistic expression. And Marshall McLuhan, referring no longer to his 'global village' but to a 'global theatre', thought advertising the 'biggest' art form of the twentieth century; the fact that it was commercial, he found irrelevant.

McLuhan praised Buckminster Fuller for trying to bridge, through his domes, the gap between visual and acoustic space. Another means to the same end has already been used on two occasions, with considerable public acclaim, by Yannis Xenakis: with the electronic music he created for the Le Corbusier pavilion at the 1967

World Exhibition in Brussels, and with his 'Polytopes de Cluny' introduced at the 1975 Festival Estival de Paris.

The latter, indeed, represented a new form of *son et lumière*, in which the pattern of the electronic score created by Xenakis was matched by an elaborate laser-beam light-show linking different points of the architectural structure of the flamboyant Gothic church of Cluny. Not for nothing was Xenakis, the composer, trained in architecture and worked as an assistant to Le Corbusier.

Symptomatic of our almost instinctive interest in the convergence of the arts is the language we use in our attempts to describe an artistic expression – and impression: a colour that 'sings' and the 'colour' of a voice, the 'rhythm' of an architectural feature and the 'architecture' of a fugue, the 'shape' of a melody, a rhythmic 'pattern', an orchestral 'texture', a 'monumental' work.

There is such 'music' in great poetry that many a composer has been accused of impertinence in setting it. Fortunately, however, examples abound of composers who have, quite undeterred, proceeded to create equivalent masterpieces by adding music to poetry or prose.

Rarer are the cases where a composer has been inspired to write music to a painting or piece of sculpture. Mussorgsky's *Tableaux d'une exposition* spring to mind in this connection.

'The artist is a dreamer' writes Gloria Morris. But a practical one, too, who possesses the skills and has acquired the craftsmanship to give physical or aural shape to his or her artistic concept.

A self-confessed amateur, but one who has gone to the root of things, Gloria Morris has about her something of the Renaissance patron of the arts. She appears to have both an innate gift of articulateness in several art forms and the ability and self-discipline necessary to learn the techniques with which to express herself through them. Today it is poetry and sculpture; tomorrow, no doubt, it will be prose and music – music, in which her patronage has so far been most positively felt.

Since Gloria Morris is entirely self-taught, hers is an excellent example of the triumph of mind over matter – precisely over the kind of matter she so aptly describes in her own preface.

Jack Bornoff
Executive Secretary of the
International Music Council of UNESCO
July 1977

INTRODUCTION

*A culture is only as great
as its dreams and its dreams
are dreamed by artists.*

L. Ron Hubbard, SCIENCE OF SURVIVAL

THROUGHOUT HISTORY MAN
has searched for answers to the questions: Where did we come from? Who are we?
Where are we going? He formulated his ideas on his relationship to the physical
universe according to the answers he found. These are the ideas which have united
him into groups and on which man has built his religions, his cultures, and his
societies.

Man's thoughts about life are constantly changing, and his dreams about his
ideal society evolve as he finds new answers to his questions.

The artist is a dreamer. He gathers the world in a dream and the dream becomes a
reality; civilizations are born, flourish and die, to give way to the new answers of
the new dreamers.

Artistic expression is a record of man's thoughts about the universe in which he
lives. They are a record of his dreams, made tangible, in the form of poems, paint-
ings, sculptures, literature, music, or philosophy. In this sense, the artist is a
philosopher and the philosopher is an artist of ideas. Their artistic expression is the
full-blown flower of their spiritual awareness.

The creative dreamer stands outside the world, outside history. He looks down
upon himself and draws the essential facts out of his experiences, his perceptions,
his knowledge, and his awareness, and forms them into images.

The *Random House Dictionary of the English Language* defines creative imagination as
'the power of recombining former experiences in the creation of new images directed
at a specific goal'.

We hear a lot of talk these days about creativity. Journalists talk about it, psy-
chologists talk about it, university professors talk about it. It seems that the only
one who does not talk about it is the artist – he doesn't have time!

An artist creates something that communicates his ideas, and hundreds of years later people talk about how he did it. They talk about his technique, his brush strokes, his counterpoint and harmonies, his use of marble, or clay, or his 'iambic pentameter'; and they give names to the techniques which became *the* technique. But the schools that follow the master never equal the master.

Then along comes another artist, and he ignores all the rules set down by the generations before him. He uses any or all techniques and invents new ones in order to communicate his ideas. He creates an emotional effect, and the cycle starts all over again.

What is forgotten is that the basic goal of an artist, and the basic purpose of art, is to communicate.

Too often today we are confronted with art that is abstruse, complex, strange, or confusing, which is meant to be accepted, not understood. Indeed, that no one understands it is often regarded as a recommendation.

If art is to communicate, however, it must, to a certain extent, be understood. This does not eliminate originality, but it does preclude incomprehensibility in the name of originality.

We often hear the expression 'When all is said and done', or 'It's all been said and done'. Of course everything has not been said and everything has not been done. Life is too full of change for that. And art takes life as its theme; even when life seems to have no theme beyond animal existence.

Art is a reality because it is the record of what we feel and know: of what we are, or what we aspire to be.

Man is a spiritual being. That thought offers a vision and a reality of an ideal existence. It tends toward health and happiness and well-being – now and in the future.

The knowledge that man is a spiritual being has existed for thousands of years, indeed, it is the oldest human concept. [1] But as our world has become more 'civilized', this knowledge has been lost. We have freed ourselves from 'superstition', or so we believe, but in the process we have lost our spiritual values and become isolated from our spiritual identity. As scientific understanding has grown, so our world has become dehumanized. Too many people today know the price of everything and the value of nothing.

A civilization based on the spirituality of man does not believe in violence, force, coercion, or resentment, because all these things react on the doer. Man is not so much punished for his evil deeds as he is punished *by* them.

Our lives are shaped by cause and effect, and the causes are to a large degree in our own hands. We are today the result of what we were yesterday, and will be tomorrow the result of what we do today.

If man is to be free, he must free himself – each individual for himself – for no one can do it for him.

If we are imprisoned, we are our own gaolers. We have forged our own bars, and we have great faith in them because we created them. What would happen if the prisoners lost faith in their bars?

[1]*In Polynesia known as* Mana. *It is referred to by some of the Greek philosophers when they speak of thought as opposed to the physical body. In Christianity it is known as Soul or Spirit. The Essence of Man. The incorporeal part of man as opposed to matter.*

Well, the fact is, many have done so; and the bars are not so strong as we think. Man has not always lived in the dark and gloom of war, insanity, and fear. There have been great moments in our history and pre-history.

So long as we are convinced that we are material animals, and that human dignity and self-respect are unattainable, we can be imprisoned. So long as we believe that our destiny is in the hands of others, we can be enslaved. So long as we believe that understanding, happiness and good health are romantic notions, *passé*, or utopian idealism, we can be victims.

Man does have the power to decide and shape his own destiny. He is capable of greatness. He has the right to aspire to that greatness. He has the right to the knowledge and wisdom that will help him shape his destiny and achieve greatness. He has the right to the awareness that he is a spiritual being.

This is the subject of my Imaginary Images.

The poems and sculptures included here reflect man's relationship to himself, to his family and friends, to mankind, to nature, to the physical universe, and to the universe of thought.

If I have spoken of man's crimes, or laughed at certain traits or ideas that some have, I have not done so in scorn.

How would I know that the state of man is tragic, and yet absurd, if I had not looked into my own heart and seen the evolution of man reflected there? The things I saw, I was. The things I see, I am.

CONCERNING THEORY

The things I see, I express in my work. I portray the realities of feelings, emotions, moods, intentions, and ideas in relation to matter, energy, space, and time.

Although I did not study art or sculpture or poetry at a university or art school, I have spent much of my life in the study of philosophy and artistic expression, and have at various times tried my hand at most of the arts. As a result, I have developed a theory of artistic expression and a very specific application of it in the sculptures. The theory is as follows.

An artist communicates by assigning time and space to matter or energy. This would be true of any artist – painter, sculptor, poet, writer, or composer.

The painter assigns space and time to matter when he puts paint on the canvas. His choice of colours and their position determine the amount of space or time he wishes to devote to any element in his painting.

The sculptor does likewise by the placement in space of clay, bronze, marble, and so on. His choice of position and size determines the amount of space and time his forms will occupy.

The composer assigns space and time to his tones (energy) when he decides the duration and alternation of sound in silence. Music can be described as the arrangement of sound in silence. But it is the choice of the arrangement that determines the quality of the music.

The writer does the same thing when he chooses his words and places them on paper. When his words are spoken he, like the composer, is working with both matter and energy, since his work consists of both sound and the materials with which it is written down.

Energy may be considered to be any sound made by an instrument or the voice. Thought and emotion are energies underlying all creative expression, both at the time of creation by the artist and at the time of perceiving (seeing, hearing, touching, etc.) by the public.

Matter may be considered to be anything material which is used, for example: paint, canvas, stone, marble, clay, metal, or symbols such as words or notes written down on paper.

The choices that an artist makes in assigning time and space to matter or energy determine his style.

The artist's skill in assigning time and space determines the quality of his communication.

The emotional response evoked from the public by the artist's work determines the effectiveness of his communication.

Time is determined by the distance, or the amount of space, between two or more points, at any given or agreed-upon speed of motion.

The more space there is between the points, the longer the time; conversely, the less space there is, the shorter the time.

Rhythm is created by reducing and increasing the space between two or more points.

An artist can create rhythm in his work, therefore, by assigning more or less space between the various points of his creation. This is also one way of building tension.

Harmony[2] is created by eliminating the space between two or more points so that these points share the same space and exist in the same unit of time.

This is best demonstrated in music. Single sounds, or notes, played alternately create a rhythm. As the space between the notes becomes smaller, the rhythm becomes faster, until the two notes are sounded together and become a chord – or harmony.

Harmony is agreement and affinity. Two or more points appearing or sounding in the same unit of time, in agreement about sharing the same space, can be said to be harmonious.

Two or more points appearing or sounding in the same unit of time, but not in agreement about sharing the same space, can be said to be dissonant.[3]

In the visual arts, the time the eye stays in the same place may be considered a unit of time. When the eye moves to another point of the work, that is another unit of time.

In prose or poetry, each image produced by a word or group of words may be considered a unit of time. One of the differences between prose and poetry is that there are fewer units of time in poetry than in prose. It takes fewer words to create an image in poetry than it does in prose. The idea is expressed in fewer words. The prose writer can use paragraphs, pages, or chapters to create an image, but

[2]Harmony is agreement or accord; a constant, orderly, or pleasing arrangement of parts; congruity. In music, any combination of tones; chordal structures as distinguished from melody and rhythm. From the Greek harmo(s), join, + ia.

[3]Dissonance is disagreement or incongruity; an inharmonious or harsh sound.

the poet must choose each word so that the image is created by small groups of words.

Rhythm can be harmonious or dissonant. Textures, colours, and forms, words and sounds and ideas, can be harmonious or dissonant.

Tension and interest are built into a work of art by the use of rhythms, harmonies, and dissonances.

The ethics of the artist also play a role in how he handles time and space in his works. Too much space makes a work disconnected and disperses the attention and interest of the viewer or listener. The points are too far apart and the tension breaks.

Too little space makes a work massive and heavy and confuses the viewer or listener. He is being confronted with too much mass and is overwhelmed.

The final product is therefore dependent on the integrity of choice and the ability of the artist to assign time and space to matter or energy. This is what has generally been called technique.

ABOUT SCULPTURE

I have applied this theory in choosing the forms and textures which I have incorporated in the sculptures.

Fragments of natural objects are incorporated in juxtaposition to the human body to create emotional and metaphysical effects. The natural elements, such as leaves, flowers, minerals, are often larger than the human figure in order to show the importance of the bond between mankind, nature, and the finite universe; a relationship which is necessary in order for them all to survive.

The human body and the natural elements are used to create images of the universe of thought, which is never shown materially. Instead it is implied by the position of the figures in relation to the natural elements with which they are associated; in other words, by the amount of space between the figures and the natural elements, or the space surrounding their respective parts.

None of the works are portraits. I do not use live models, but observe life, in both its physical and emotional aspects. When I first began to work as a sculptor, I worked exclusively in wax. Then I began to combine wax and clay. Most of the works shown in this book are of the second period.

The human figures are, for the most part, created in clay. The natural elements are first treated with wax, then combined with the clay figures. Most of the elements with heavy texture were done in wax.

The casting technique is a combination of standard moulding techniques from original clay models. The natural objects are invested[4] in their natural or wax state.

The sculptures are built up combining the natural objects and the human figures, either at the stage before casting when the figure is in wax, or after casting when both the figure and the natural objects are in bronze or silver.

This system of casting was developed with the co-operation of Eric Gibbard, Dennis Ball and Ted Knell, now foundry directors of the Burleighfield International Art Centre in Loadwater, Buckinghamshire.

[4]*Investment casting is a casting process in which an expendable pattern is surrounded by an 'investment' compound and then baked so that*

the investment is hardened
to form a mould and the
pattern material may be
burnt or melted away and
run off.

[5] *The wax shop is where
clay models are cast into
wax models before being cast
in metal. This is known
as the lost wax process.
The wax model is invested
and the wax is melted
away in baking. Liquid
metal is then poured into the
cavity left by the wax.*

[6] *Chasing is the finishing
of the metalwork by cutting
drilling, grinding, filing,
and finally polishing. It
takes the rough-cast
sculpture from the time it
is taken out of the mould
up to the final stage of
patinating.*

[7] *Patina is a coloration
or incrustation produced
on bronze by natural
oxidization or by the
application of chemicals.
It turns the bronze green,
brown, blue, etc.,
depending on the chemicals
used.*

[8] *In painting, for example,
there is the brush between
the hand of the artist and
the canvas. With musical
instruments such as the
piano or the violin, there
are keys or a bow between
the hands of the performer and
the music. But with the
guitar and the harp the*

For two years I worked with the craftsmen at the Morris Singer Foundry, where most of these works were cast. I was able to follow the works from the wax shop,[5] through the casting, and into the chasing[6] shop, where I worked with the chaser and did all my own patinas.[7]

It was necessary to make many casts of each of the natural materials in order to obtain the final result. The reason for this is that in direct investment and lost wax casting there is no mould. The original model is burnt away during the baking of the investment, and once the works are cast the original model is lost. If all or part of a piece does not run, the entire work is lost. With this method each work is therefore unique and no copies or editions can be made.

Casting natural materials together with models originally made in clay has never, to our knowledge, been done before, and it was only possible thanks to the special relationship with the foundry. There were enormous risks, as neither I nor the foundry knew beforehand which pieces would be successful and which would not. Many new techniques were developed during these two years.

For me, these were my two most valuable years as a sculptor. The knowledge, technique, and experience could only have been acquired in a foundry. These are things that one cannot learn in a school of fine art. The actual practical problems of creating a bronze sculpture are handled in the foundry – not in the artist's studio or in a classroom. It is in the foundry that the mistakes of the sculptor are handled or corrected. The mistakes are not limited to the amateur. Well-known sculptors also give casting problems to the foundry. Solving these problems is part of the job of a good art foundry, and working in close co-operation with good craftsmen has given me an insight into the craft of sculpture-making that would not otherwise have been possible.

A sculpture in bronze, or any cast metal, is created by the inspiration of the artist combined with the skill of the foundry craftsman. There must be understanding, a shared reality, and clear communication between the two. If these things do not exist, it will show in the work. The craftsman is not the artist, and yet without him the artist's inspiration could not be realized in metal.

Not all sculptors want to work like this, and not all foundries allow it; but when it is possible, it is to everyone's advantage, and a better final product is the result. The hand of the craftsman becomes an extension of the hand of the artist.

Sculpture is essentially a tactile art. Working in clay is rather like playing the guitar, in that there is no intermediary between the hand of the artist and the final product.[8]

The tactile perceptions often tell me more than the visual perceptions. For this reason, I seldom use tools. The size of the work does not alter the perception. If it is a large work, the hands have large perceptions. If it is a small work, the hands seem to become small and the perceptions are all small.

With the use of mirrors I can work on all sides of the sculpture simultaneously, and thereby obviate either a 'front' or 'back'.

Because sculpture is both tactile and three-dimensional, I believe that it should be touched as well as viewed. Because the forms are real, and not just visual allusions

20

to texture and roundness, sculpture should be as emotional, harmonious or dissonant to the touch as to the eye. It should communicate through the visual and the tactile perceptions.

In galleries that exhibit sculpture, wouldn't it be nice to see signs that read PLEASE TOUCH?

hand of the artist creates the sound directly. Clay sculpture is basically the same thing.

INTRODUCTION

*La grandeur d'une culture est
à la mesure de ses rêves; or,
ces rêves sont rêvés par les artistes.*

L. Ron Hubbard SCIENCE OF SURVIVAL

Au COURS DE L'HISTOIRE
l'homme a cherché les réponses aux questions: 'D'où venons-nous? Qui sommes-nous? Où allons-nous?' Il a formulé sa pensée sur ses rapports avec l'univers physique selon les réponses qu'il a trouvées. Ce sont les idées qui ont regroupé les hommes et selon lesquelles l'homme a construit ses religions, ses cultures et ses sociétés.

Les idées qu'a l'homme sur la vie changent continuellement; ses rêves d'une société idéale évoluent au fur et à mesure qu'il trouve de nouvelles réponses à ses questions.

L'artiste, 'ce rêveur définitif' (André Breton, *Manifeste du Surréalisme*), cueille le monde dans un rêve et le rêve devient réalité. Les civilisations naissent, s'épanouissent et meurent, pour s'effacer devant les nouvelles réponses des nouveaux rêveurs.

L'expression artistique est un témoignage de la pensée de l'homme sur l'univers dans lequel il vit – un témoignage de ses rêves, devenus tangibles, sous forme de poésie, de tableaux, de sculpture, de littérature, de musique ou de philosophie.

Dans ce sens, l'artiste est un philosophe, et le philosophe est un artiste de la pensée. Leurs expressions artistiques sont les fleurs épanouies de leurs consciences.

L'artiste rêveur se tient en dehors du monde et de l'histoire. De là, il se regarde et tire les faits essentiels de son expérience, de sa sensibilité, de sa connaissance et de son niveau de conscience, et il en fait des images.

Le *Random House Dictionary of the English Language* définit l'imagination créatrice comme étant 'l'aptitude à rassembler les expériences antérieures en vue de créer de nouvelles images avec un but spécifique.'

De nos jours, on parle beaucoup de la créativité. Les journalistes en parlent, les psychologues en parlent et les professeurs de facultés aussi. On dirait que le seul qui n'en parle pas, c'est l'artiste lui-même – il n'en a pas le temps!

23

Le créateur communique sa pensée à travers ses oeuvres, et quelques siècles plus tard, on se met à discuter la façon dont il les a faites. On étudie sa technique : sa touche, son contrepoint et ses harmonies, son utilisation du marbre, des métaux ou de la terre glaise, ou de ses alexandrins. On attribue alors un nom à ces techniques qui deviennent la technique par excellence. Toutefois, les écoles qui suivent le maître n'atteignent jamais son niveau.

Plus tard, un autre artiste naît et il se met à ignorer tous les préceptes des générations précédentes. Il choisit soit une, soit plusieurs, soit toutes les techniques, ou même rien du tout, et en invente des nouvelles afin de communiquer sa pensée. Il provoque une réaction des émotions et le cycle recommence.

Ce qu'on oublie souvent c'est que le but fondamental de l'artiste, et le but fondamental de l'art même, est de communiquer, dans le sens le plus élevé du mot.

Trop souvent aujourd'hui, on se trouve confronté par un art qui est touffu, compliqué, étrange ou confus et qui demande à être accepté, mais non pas à être compris. De la sorte, le fait d'être incompris est souvent considéré comme une recommandation en lui-même.

Donc, si l'art doit communiquer, il doit, dans une certaine mesure, être compris. Cela n'élimine pas l'originalité mais, forcément, il écarte toute incompréhension dans l'intérêt même de cette originalité.

Nous entendons souvent l'expression 'on l'a déjà dit,' ou 'c'est du déjà vu'. Il est évident pourtant qu'on n'a pas encore tout dit ni tout fait. La vie est trop remplie de changements pour que cela arrive. Elle est l'inspiration de l'art, même quand elle ne semble avoir aucune signification.

L'art est une réalité, un témoignage de nos sentiments et de nos connaissances – de ce que nous sommes et de ce que nous voulons atteindre.

Le concept que l'homme est un esprit puissant présente une image et une réalité d'une existence idéale. Il aspire à la santé, au bonheur et au bien-être, à présent et dans l'avenir.

Il y a des millénaires, l'homme était conscient qu'il était un esprit puissant : ce fut un des concepts les plus anciens de la civilisation humaine.[1] Or, au fur et à mesure que notre monde est devenu plus 'civilisé', cette connaissance s'est perdue. Nous nous sommes libérés des 'superstitions', du moins c'est ce que nous croyons, mais entretemps, nous avons perdu notre sens de la valeur humaine et nous nous sommes isolés de notre identité spirituelle. Plus la science s'est développée et plus notre monde est devenu inhumain. Trop de gens aujourd'hui connaissent le prix de tout, mais la valeur de rien.

Une civilisation basée sur l'identité spirituelle de l'homme n'admet pas la violence, la force, la contrainte, ou la rancune, puisque celles-ci rebondissent sur l'individu qui les a provoquées. L'homme n'est pas tant puni pour ses méfaits qu'il est puni *par* eux.

Notre vie est façonnée par des relations de cause à effet, et les causes sont, dans une grande mesure, entre nos mains. Aujourd'hui, nous sommes le résultat de ce que nous étions hier et nous serons demain le résultat de ce que nous sommes aujourd'hui.

Si l'homme se veut libre, il doit se libérer lui-même, car nul autre ne peut le faire à sa place.

[1] Il s'agit, chez les chrétiens, de l'âme, ou de l'esprit. L'essence de l'Homme. La partie incorporelle de l'homme par rapport à la matière. Certains philosophes grecs y ont fait allusion lorsqu'ils ont parlé de la pensée par rapport au corps. Les Polynésiens l'appellent 'Mana'.

Si nous nous trouvons emprisonnés, c'est que nous sommes nos propres geôliers. Nous avons forgé nos propres barreaux et nous leur accordons toute notre confiance puisque nous les avons créés. Que se passerait-il si les prisonniers perdaient la foi en leur barreaux?

Or, beaucoup l'ont fait et ils ont découvert que les barreaux ne sont pas aussi solides qu'ils le croyaient. L'homme n'a pas toujours vécu dans la tristesse d'une guerre sombre, ni dans la folie ou dans la peur. Il y a eu bien des moments de grandeur au cours de notre histoire et de notre préhistoire.

Tant que nous restons convaincus que nous ne sommes que des corps, à un niveau animal, et que la dignité humaine et le respect de soi sont hors de portée, il sera possible de nous emprisonner. Tant que nous croyons fermement que notre destin se trouve entre les mains des autres, il sera possible de nous réduire à l'esclavage. Tant que nous croyons que la compréhension, le bonheur, et la santé ne sont que des notions romanesques désuètes ou de l'idéalisme utopique, nous en serons les victimes.

L'homme a le pouvoir de décider et de forger son propre destin. Il est capable de grandeur d'âme. Il a le droit d'aspirer à la connaissance et à la sagesse qui l'aideront à façonner son destin et à atteindre cette grandeur. Il a le droit d'être conscient de son identité spirituelle.

Voici donc le sujet de mes *Images Imaginaires*.

Les poèmes et les sculptures dans ce livre sont un reflet du rapport de l'Homme avec lui-même, avec sa famille et ses amis, avec l'Humanité toute entière, avec la nature, avec l'univers physique et avec l'univers de la pensée.

Si j'ai parlé des méfaits de l'homme, ou ri de certaines de ses caractéristiques ou de ses idées, je ne l'ai pas fait par mépris.

Comment aurais-je pu savoir que la condition de l'homme est tragique, et pourtant absurde, si je n'avais pas regardé dans mon propre coeur et vu l'évolution de l'homme qui y est reflétée. Ce que j'ai vu, je l'ai été. Ce que je vois, je le suis.

PROPOS SUR LA THEORIE

Ce que je vois, je l'exprime dans mes oeuvres. Je dépeins les réalités des sentiments, des émotions, des intentions et des idées en rapport avec la matière, l'énergie, l'espace et le temps.

Je n'ai étudié ni l'art, ni la sculpture, ni la poésie, en faculté ou aux Beaux Arts. Pourtant, j'ai passé beaucoup de temps à étudier la philosophie et l'expression artistique; j'ai expérimenté, à plusieurs reprises, avec la plupart des formes artistiques. Il en est résulté une théorie d'expression artistique dont ma sculpture est l'application spécifique, et qui est la suivante.

Afin de communiquer, l'artiste attribue le temps et l'espace à la matière ou à l'énergie. Ceci est vrai pour n'importe quel artiste: peintre, sculpteur, poète, écrivain ou compositeur.

Le peintre attribue l'espace et le temps à la matière quand il applique la peinture sur ses toiles. Son choix de couleurs et de leur position détermine l'espace ou le temps qu'il désire donner à tout élément de son tableau.

Le sculpteur fait de même en déplaçant, dans l'espace, la terre glaise, le bronze, le marbre, etc. Son choix de la position et de la taille détermine l'espace et le temps que ses formes prendront.

Le compositeur attribue l'espace et le temps à ses tonalités (l'énergie) quand il décide de la durée et de l'alternance des sons dans le silence. On peut définir la musique comme étant un arrangement de sons dans le silence. Toutefois, c'est le choix de l'agencement qui détermine la qualité de la musique.

L'écrivain fait de même lorsqu'il choisit ses mots et les couche sur le papier. Quand ses écrits sont lus à haute voix, tel le compositeur, il manie à la fois la matière et l'énergie, car son oeuvre est composée de sons mais aussi du matériel avec lequel elle a été transcrite sur papier.

On peut considérer l'énergie comme étant un son, émis par un instrument, ou par la voix. La pensée et les émotions sont des énergies qui sous-tendent toute expression artistique, au moment même de la création par l'artiste et au moment de sa perception (voir, écouter, toucher, etc.) par le public.

On peut considérer la matière comme un matériau qui est utilisé – tel que la peinture, la toile, la pierre, le marbre, la terre glaise, le métal – ou des symboles, tels que les notes ou les mots, écrits.

Le choix que fait l'artiste en attribuant le temps et l'espace à la matière ou à l'énergie détermine son style.

L'aptitude de l'artiste à attribuer ce temps et cet espace détermine la qualité de sa communication.

Les sentiments éveillés chez le public par l'oeuvre de l'artiste déterminent l'efficacité de sa communication.

Le temps est délimité par la distance, ou l'espace qu'il y a entre deux ou plusieurs points, à toute vitesse de mouvement donnée, ou prédéterminée.

Plus il y a de l'espace entre les points, plus le temps est long; inversement, plus l'espace est réduit, plus le temps est court.

Un rythme est créé en diminuant et en augmentant l'espace entre deux ou plusieurs points.

De la sorte, l'artiste peut donner un rythme à son oeuvre en attribuant plus ou moins d'espace entre les points de sa création. C'est également une des façons de créer la tension.

Une harmonie[2] est établie en éliminant l'espace entre deux ou plusieurs points pour que ces points puissent partager le même espace et exister dans la même unité de temps. La musique en est la meilleure preuve.

Les sons isolés, ou les notes, joués alternativement, créent un rythme. Quand l'espace entre deux notes se réduit, le rythme s'accélère, jusqu'à ce que les deux notes soient entendues simultanément et deviennent un accord, ou une harmonie.

L'harmonie est donc accord et affinité. Deux ou plusieurs points qui apparaissent ou qui résonnent dans la même unité de temps, en accord pour partager le même espace, sont dits 'harmonieux'.

[2]Harmonie : accord ou concorde ; accord entre les éléments d'un tout ; consonnant. En musique, tout accord de divers sons ; tout groupe de notes peut se faire entendre de deux façons : soit successivement, soit simultanément. Dans

Deux ou plusieurs points qui apparaissent ou qui résonnent dans la même unité de temps, mais non en accord pour partager le même espace, sont dits 'dissonants'.[3]

Dans l'art plastique, le temps que l'oeil met à rester au même endroit peut être considéré comme une unité. Lorsque l'oeil passe à un autre point de l'oeuvre, c'est une autre unité de temps.

En prose ou en vers, chaque image produite par un mot ou par un groupe de mots peut être considérée comme une unité de temps. L'une des différences entre la prose et la poésie réside dans le fait qu'il y a moins d'unités de temps en poésie qu'en prose. Il faut moins de mots pour créer une image en vers qu'il n'en faut en prose. L'idée est exprimée en moins de mots. L'écrivain de prose tient à sa disposition des paragraphes, des pages ou des chapitres pour créer une image, mais le poète est obligé de soupeser chaque mot afin que l'image soit créée par de tout petits groupes de mots.

Un rythme peut être harmonieux ou dissonant. La texture, les couleurs, les formes, les mots, les sons et les idées peuvent être harmonieux ou dissonants. La tension et l'intérêt sont construits dans l'oeuvre par l'utilisation des rythmes, des harmonies et des dissonances. L'éthique de l'artiste joue également un rôle selon la manière dont il manie le temps et l'espace dans son oeuvre. Trop d'espace rend une oeuvre décousue et disperse l'attention et l'intérêt du public. Les points sont trop éloignés et la tension est rompue.

Trop peu d'espace rend une oeuvre volumineuse et lourde. Le public est donc troublé parce qu'il est confronté par une masse trop écrasante.

L'oeuvre, une fois terminée, dépend donc de l'intégrité du choix et de la capacité de l'artiste d'attribuer le temps et l'espace à la matière ou à l'énergie. C'est ce qui, d'une manière générale, est appelé technique.

LA SCULPTURE

J'ai appliqué cette théorie dans mon choix des formes et de la texture incorporées dans mes oeuvres.

Des fragments d'objets naturels sont placés en juxtaposition au corps humain afin de créer des effets émotionnels et métaphysiques. Les éléments naturels, tels les feuilles, les fleurs, les minéraux, sont souvent plus grands que le personnage humain afin de démontrer l'importance du lien entre l'humanité, la nature et l'univers physique – un rapport indispensable pour qu'ils survivent.

Le corps humain et les éléments naturels sont utilisés pour créer des images de l'univers de la pensée, ce qui n'est jamais montré mais est suggéré uniquement. Cet univers est sous-entendu grâce à la position des personnages par rapport aux éléments naturels avec lesquels ils sont associés; en d'autres termes, par le volume de l'espace entre les personnages et les éléments naturels, ou par l'espace qui entoure les parties intégrantes ou séparées.

Il n'y a aucun portrait. Je n'utilise pas de modèles vivants, mais j'observe la vie, tout à la fois dans ses aspects physiques et émotionnels.

le premier cas, il y a une mélodie ; dans le deuxième cas, il y a une harmonie. Du grec 'harmo', joindre.

[3]*Dissonance : désaccord, cacophonie ; un son peu harmonieux ou dur.*

4Le moulage à investissement
(encroûtement) est un
procédé par lequel un
modèle dispensable est
entouré d'un encroûtement
et ensuite cuit au four
afin de le durcir; il devient
le moule; le modèle
dispensable est soit brûlé,
soit fondu.

5L'atelier de cire perdue
est le lieu où les modèles
en terre glaise sont moulés
en cire avant d'être
moulés en métal. Le
modèle en cire est entouré
de l'encroûtement et la
cire est fondue lors de la
cuisson. Le métal liquide
est alors versé dans
l'espace laissé par la cire.

6Le ciselage est le dernier
stade du travail du métal;
il s'agit de couper, percer,
poncer, limer et finalement
de polir le métal. Ce
procédé débute au stade du
brut de fonte, au moment
où l'oeuvre est sortie du
moule, et se termine au
dernier stade, c'est-à-
dire celui de la patine.

7La patine est une
altération artificielle du
bronze lors de l'application
de produits, chimiques ou
naturels, par oxydation.
Le bronze peut devenir vert,
marron, bleu, etc. selon
les produits chimiques
utilisés.

Au début, quand j'ai commencé à sculpter, je n'utilisais que la cire; ensuite, j'ai associé la cire à la terre glaise. La plupart des oeuvres de ce livre sont de la seconde periode.

Les personnages sont, pour la plupart, réalisés en terre glaise. Les éléments naturels sont, en premier lieu, traités à la cire; ensuite, les deux parties sont assemblées. La plupart des éléments à texture rugueuse ont été traités à la cire.

Le moulage a été effectué selon des méthodes classiques à partir des modèles d'origine. Les éléments naturels sont investis[4] dans leur état naturel ou dans la cire.

Les différentes parties de l'oeuvre sont assemblées, soit avant le moulage, avec le personnage en cire, soit après le moulage quand le personnage et les éléments naturels sont déjà en bronze ou en argent.

Ce système de moulage a été développé en association avec Eric Gibbard, Dennis Ball, et Ted Knell, nouveaux directeurs du Burleighfield International Art Centre à Loudwater, Buckinghamshire, Grande-Bretagne.

J'ai travaillé pendant deux ans avec les artisans de la Morris Singer Foundry où la plupart de ces oeuvres ont été moulées. De la sorte, je les ai suivies de l'atelier de cire perdu,[5] au moulage, et enfin, à l'atelier de ciselage[6] ou j'ai travaillé avec le ciseleur et patiné[7] moi-même mes oeuvres.

Il était nécessaire de faire plusieurs moulages de chaque élément afin d'obtenir le résultat définitif. La raison en est que lors de l'investissement direct et le procédé de cire perdu, le modèle original est incinéré et perdu. Si une ou toutes les parties ne sortent pas du moule, l'oeuvre est entièrement perdue. Chacune d'elles est donc unique et aucune édition ne peut en être faite.

A notre connaissance, c'est la première fois que des matériaux naturels ont été moulés en association avec des modèles en terre glaise. Cela a été rendu possible grâce à l'entente rare qui a existé entre nous tous. Les risques à prendre étaient énormes puisque ni moi-même, ni la fonderie ne savait, par avance, quelles étaient les pièces qui en sortiraient. De la sorte, au cours de ces deux années, nous avons eu l'occasion de développer de nouvelles techniques.

C'était, pour moi, deux années très édifiantes en tant que sculpteur. Ce n'est qu'à la fonderie elle-même qu'on arrive à acquérir cette connaissance, cette technique et cette expérience. Ce sont des choses que l'on ne peut pas apprendre à l'école. Les problèmes pratiques de la création d'un bronze sont résolus à la fonderie – et non pas à l'atelier même de l'artiste ou aux Beaux Arts, par exemple. C'est à la fonderie que les erreurs du sculpteur sont corrigées. L'amateur n'a donc pas la priorité aux erreurs. Les sculpteurs célèbres posent également des problèmes aux fondeurs. Il est évident que la résolution de ces problèmes fait partie du travail d'une bonne fonderie. Le fait d'avoir pu travailler en étroite collaboration avec d'excellents artisans m'a permis de connaître la technologie des artisans-fondeurs.

Un bronze, ou toute autre sculpture moulée, est le résultat de l'inspiration de l'artiste, associée à l'adresse de l'artisan-fondeur. Il faut donc qu'une parfaite compréhension existe entre les deux, de même qu'une réalité partagée et une communication précise. Sans elles, l'oeuvre s'en ressentirait. L'artisan n'est pas l'artiste et pourtant, sans lui, l'inspiration de l'artiste ne pourrait jamais être réalisée.

Peut-être cette méthode ne convient-elle pas à tous les sculpteurs ; de même, toutes les fonderies ne la permettraient pas non plus – mais elle est souhaitable dans l'intérêt de l'oeuvre. La main de l'artisan devient une extension de celle de l'artiste.

La sculpture est, au fond, un art tactile. Le travail de la terre glaise ressemble au jeu de la guitare en ce sens qu'il n'y a aucun intermédiaire entre la main de l'artiste et l'oeuvre définitive. [8]

Pour moi, les perceptions tactiles sont souvent plus révélatrices que les perceptions visuelles. C'est pour cette raison que j'ai rarement utilisé des outils. La taille de l'oeuvre n'influence pas cette perception car, s'il s'agit d'une oeuvre importante, les mains reçoivent des perceptions de grande taille ; de même, s'il s'agit d'une oeuvre qui est petite, les mains donnent l'impression de devenir petites et les perceptions reçues sont, elles aussi, petites.

Je travaille les deux faces de mes sculptures simultanément, en utilisant un jeu de miroirs, ce qui fait que je peux voir tous les angles en même temps et qu'il n'y a de ce fait pas de côté prédominant.

Etant donné que la sculpture est, à la fois, un art tactile et à trois dimensions, il me semble qu'il faut non seulement voir, mais également toucher les oeuvres, car elles ont des formes réelles et ne font pas ariquement illusion à une texture ou à une forme arrondie. La sculpture se doit donc de sensibiliser, de façon soit harmonieuse, soit dissonante, la main autant que l'oeil. Elle doit arriver à communiquer par les perceptions visuelles et tactiles.

Dans cet ordre d'idées, ne serait-il pas agréable de voir, dans les galeries de sculpture, des panneaux indiquant 'VOUS ETES INVITÉ À TOUCHER' ?

[8]*Dans la peinture, par exemple, le pinceau se trouve entre la main de l'artiste et sa toile. Dans le cas de certains instruments de musique, tel que le piano ou le violon, il y a des touches, ou un archet, qui se trouvent entre les mains de l'interprète et sa musique. Par contre, en ce qui concerne la guitare et la harpe, c'est la main de l'artiste lui-même qui crée la musique directement. De même, la main du sculpteur crée directement, de la terre glaise, son oeuvre.*

IMAGINARY IMAGES

A NOTE ON THE MEASUREMENTS

The measurements given of the following sculptures represent the maximum width and height without the base, the width always being given first.

PRIMO TEMPO

A Primo Tempo
The seed –
Inert potential,
Conceives the union
Between Earth and Air,
The common origin
Of man and nature.
Source of all life
Transcending the aeons,
Awaits
A new life in harmony –
A Primo Tempo.

Primo Tempo (Latin): a musical term meaning 'at the original time'.

Primo Tempo, bronze, 1974 (15 × 27 cm.)

The common origin
Of man and nature.
Source of all life
Transcending the aeons,
Awaits.

Primo Tempo (back view)

Mirrors for identity.
Those qualities of being –
Reflected.
Related and revered:
The trees and shrubs,
The sun and stars,
The wind
At greatest power, whirls.
The seasons
Change to return where they were.
Childhood to childhood.
The circle.
Sacred wisdom
To which no man is immune –
Reflected.
Forms and forces of the Universe.
Counterpart to the soul of man.

Reflection: an image, representation, or counterpart. Careful thought about something. In physics, the return of energy such as light, heat, or sound.

Mirrors for Identity, bronze, 1975 (45 ×29 cm.)

Those qualities of being –
Reflected.
Related and revered.

Reverie, bronze, 1973 (37 × 26 cm.)

Childhood to childhood.
The circle.
Sacred wisdom
To which no man is immune –
Reflected.

Reflection, bronze, 1976 (37 × 26 cm.)

Forms and forces of the Universe.
Counterpart to the soul of man.

Elements, silver and rock crystal, 1974 (17 × 17 cm.)

MANUS TERRAE

Manus Terrae
Hands of the earth,
Offering eternal
Life, through rebirth.

Rose and Sunbeam
Held in her hand.
Mystic daydream
Or, Truth of the land?

Manus Terrae, bronze, 1974 (21 × 20 cm.)

Hands of the earth,
Offering eternal
Life, through rebirth.

The Source, bronze, 1973

METAMORPHOSIS

The halls of space and spheres once rang
With echoes of a sacred song,
That all men knew, and all tongues sang;
    Held in time – aeons long.

Today, in other accents, bound
By simple truths misnamed,
Those same tongues reverse the sound
    That music once proclaimed.

Bereft of knowledge, and ineffective,
These then are the fools of time;
Immune to all, and all subjective,
Who die for beauty and live for crime.

Metamorphosis: any complete change in appearance, character, circumstances, etc.

Metamorphosis, silver, 1975 (23 ×20 cm.)

With echoes of a sacred song,
That all men knew, and all tongues sang;
Held in time – aeons long.

Stella Maris (Latin): Star of the sea.

Stella Maris, bronze, 1974 (30 × 30 cm.)

Bereft of knowledge, and ineffective,
These then are the fools of time.

Lacrimosa (Latin): tearful. A part of the Requiem Mass; used musically in the Requiems of Mozart and Verdi.

Lacrimosa, bronze, 1974 (51 × 21 cm.)

Immune to all, and all subjective,
Who die for beauty and live for crime.

Lacrimosa (back view)

WINDS OF WISDOM

In wand'ring wisps of rhythm
Ancient reflections linger
        Endlessly
Amid spacial galaxies –
And man's soul,
            Alighting
Dreams of remaining shadows
Still shifting silently.

And beauty is only an echo.

Awaken winds of wisdom
With life's reason –
        To be.
Banish doubt
And open palaces
        Of song
Where serene forces stand
Between man and magic.

Wisps of Rhythm, bronze, 1974 (40 × 14 cm.)

And man's soul,
Alighting
Dreams of remaining shadows.

Lotus Land, silver, 1974 (10 × 21.5 cm.)

And beauty is only an echo.

Unity: used in the sense of the oneness of an interconnected series. Oneness of mind, feeling, etc. as among a number of persons. Concord, agreement, or harmony.

Unity, silver, 1975 (21 × 14 cm.)

Awaken winds of wisdom
With life's reason –
To be.

Harmony, bronze, 1976

Banish doubt
And open palaces
          Of song
Where serene forces stand
Between man and magic.

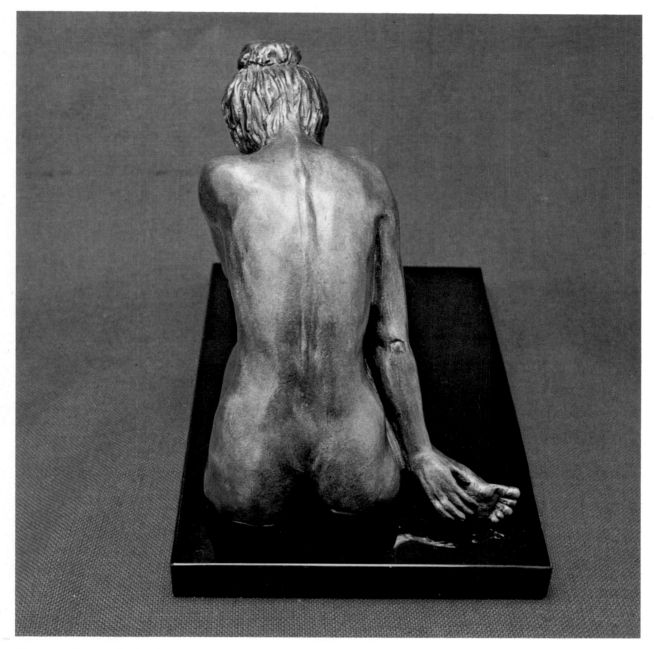

Harmony (second view)

THE MYSTERY OF MUSIC

Sound shadows wash the night
As shells upon the shore,
Echoing the serenade
That was love – before.

Through the corridors of time
In harmony with the spheres,
Drifts the primordial music
Of life – without tears.

An instant arrested in eternity
Pulsates the borders of our lives;
In rhythm with the earth
The voice of creation – survives.

Mystery of Music, bronze, 1974 (20 × 16 cm.)

In rhythm with the earth

Rhythm of the Earth, bronze, 1974 (45 × 10 cm.)

Through the corridors of time
In harmony with the spheres

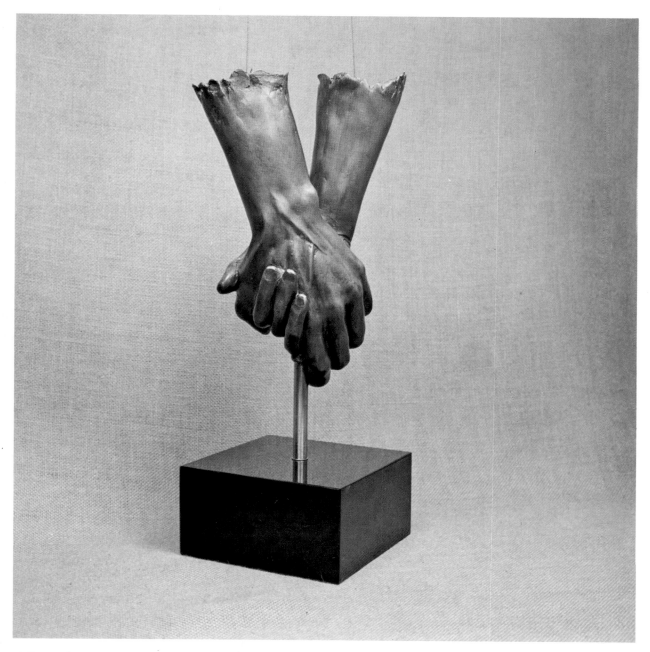

Affinity, bronze, 1976

Drifts the primordial music
Of life – without tears.

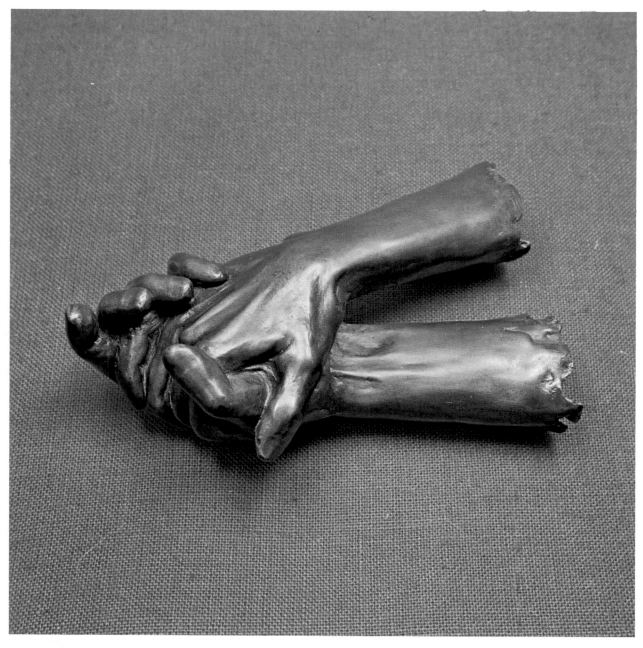

Reality, bronze, 1976

An instant arrested in eternity
Pulsates the borders of our lives;
In rhythm with the earth
The voice of creation – survives.

Communication, bronze, 1976

VULCAN'S MIRROR

Vulcan's mirror
Time's error.
Past, present and future flow
In reverse image of know;
And secret loves of long ago
In towers of silence glow.

Vulcan: the Roman god of fire and the working of metals. A son of Jupiter and Juno, he was the husband of Venus and father of Cupid.

His workshops were under Mount Etna and other volcanoes where he forged thunderbolts for Jove. He is said to have had a mirror which showed the past, the present, and the future.

Amoroso (Latin): a musical term meaning loving(ly).

Amoroso, bronze, 1975 (17 × 15 cm.)

And secret loves of long ago
In towers of silence glow.

Cathedral, bronze, 1973 (57 × 15 cm.)

AVE PHOENIX (Hail Phoenix)

At the edge of the world,
A spectator of flight;
Longing to soar
But afraid of the night.

Caressed by the moon
And wind's gentle breath,
With whispers and promises
Of life – or of death?

Oh, earthbound bird,
How high you could fly!
Take wing over rainbows
To freedom – or die.

At the edge of the world,
Respond to my call.
Take flight from oblivion
Through the Fiery Wall.

Whose is that song
So distant yet clear?
Those words of love
Compel flight without fear.

Mysterious fanfare
From a silver horn –
Out of the ashes
A new bird is born!

Ave Phoenix.

Soaring on sunbeams
To hail the morn –
Out of the ashes
A new bird is born!

Ave Phoenix.

82

Ave Phoenix, bronze, 1974 (48 × 24 cm.)

Caressed by the moon
And wind's gentle breath,
With whispers and promises

Spiritus (Latin): the life force. The vital principle of man which animates the body.
Breath of life. *Elan Vital.*

84

Spiritus, silver, 1975 (17 × 12 cm.)

Of life – or of death?

Spiritus (back view)

At the edge of the world,
Respond to my call.
Take flight from oblivion
Through the Fiery Wall.

Ave Phoenix (detail)

Whose is that song
So distant yet clear?
Those words of love
Compel flight without fear.

Listening, bronze, 1976

Mysterious fanfare
From a silver horn

(Luna) *Evocante* (Latin): call of the moon. Evoke: to produce or suggest through artistry and imagination a vivid impression of reality.

Luna Evocante, silver, 1974 (30 × 17 cm.)

Soaring on sunbeams
To hail the morn

Volition: the act of willing, choosing, or resolving; a choice or decision made by the will; determination.

Volition, bronze, 1974 (14 × 28 cm.)

Out of the ashes
A new bird is born.

Volition (back view)

In this the sunset of the soul
Silence makes no secret music,
But bells of science toll
    For Gods renamed
    And Demons defined.
    The ultimates . . .
When logic is the goal.

And truth reflects the light of power
With words of beauty measured.
In this our amber hour,
    To requiems of wind,
    In silent thunder,
    Explodes . . .
A single nocturnal flower.

Behold this brave new rose of night
Glowing of such a fire, with eyes
Of the soul's supreme sight.
    Herein lives truth,
    And beauty's wisdom,
    Proclaiming . . .
All that was and is, tonight.

This flame alone, to life, gives light.

Silent Thunder, bronze, 1976

Silence makes no secret music
But bells of science toll

Song of Sadness, bronze, 1973

For Gods renamed
And Demons defined

Demon: from the Greek *daimonion* – a thing of divine nature. In modern usage it is defined as an evil spirit, devil. In ancient Greek, a supernatural intelligence; a guardian spirit, genius. A person of great energy and skill.

102

Fantasia, bronze, 1975 (38 × 21 cm.)

In this our amber hour,
        To requiems of wind,
        In silent thunder

. . . .

This flame alone, to life, gives light.

St Francis Walking on the Waves is based on the story of St Francis, who came to the water's edge and was refused transport across by the boatman, whereupon he hurled his cloak on the waters and crossed, with only a symbol of his faith, which he held in his hand. The legend is that it was his faith in himself and in God that made it possible to survive the storm and arrive safely on the other side.

Franz Liszt was inspired by a painting of this legend, and told it musically in his piano work of the same title (*St François Marchant sur les Flots*).

St Francis Walking on the Waves, bronze, 1976

Behold this brave new rose of night
Glowing of such a fire, with eyes
Of the soul's supreme sight.
            Herein lives truth
            And beauty's wisdom,
            Proclaiming . . .
All that was and is, tonight.

Silent Thunder (second view)

NOTES ON THE POEMS

Primo Tempo is the beginning. All the potentials of man, nature, and the universe, in essence, not matter, await a new birth.

Mirrors for Identity is based on several concepts of reflection. The first is reflection as in profound thought.

The second is the reflection, or image, produced by a mirror; the intangible counterpart of the material thing. These are images, like thought, which are related, but remain abstract.

The third is reflection as it is understood in physics; energy, such as light, heat, or sound, returns after striking a surface. Crystals reflect light, metal reflects heat, and a person can reflect the thoughts of another.

Manus Terrae is Latin, meaning 'hands of the earth'. The hands of the earth represent the spiritual source of all that exists. The theme is similar to that of *Primo Tempo*.

Metamorphosis is about the complete change in man's state of being. It refers to that most ancient concept that has been passed down from father to son, by word of mouth, in music and in words – that man is a spiritual being. Today that knowledge, which was once sacred, has become profane. Even the words and symbols have changed and are now misunderstood.

For example, Pan. The word 'pan' in ancient Greek means 'all', as in 'pancromatic' (all colours) or 'panorama' (over-all view). Pan was a god of nature and fertility – a god of all living things. He was pictured with the head, chest, and arms of a man and the legs of a goat, cloven-hooved, and with horns. This symbol of life was changed: by the addition of a forked tail and the colour red, Pan became the Devil.

The word 'demon' comes from the Greek *diamonion*, which means a thing of divine nature. Today it means an evil spirit.

Even the word 'spirit' has changed. Today it is used interchangeably with ghost, phantom, or other things that go bump in the night.

These are only a few of the concepts that were once sacred, but are now profane.

In *Metamorphosis*, as in all the poems, 'Music' is used in its pre-Pythagorean sense. Pythagoras was a Greek thinker, mathematician, astronomer, and religious reformer. He invented the Major scale in music. The word 'philosophy' was not known before Pythagoras's time. It was included in the word 'music', which means 'art or science of the Muse'.

The word 'music' was used comprehensively for all the arts of the Nine Muses,[1] and included the concept of thought, or soul, as distinguished from the body. The singing and setting of lyric poetry was only a small, but central, part of a 'musical' education. Music included reading, writing, the sciences of mathematics and astronomy, besides all the arts of literature. Music was valued both in its original, general sense and in the modern, restricted sense, chiefly as an educational element in the formation of character, thought, or soul.

When this concept is suppressed or falls into disuse, there is a *Metamorphosis* of the thoughts and actions of man. What sort of wisdom is it that says one should die or suffer for beauty? And yet how many martyrs have died in the name of 'good' and beauty? How many times have we heard 'Great art is only created out of great suffering'? How many of our great creative artists have lived and died in misery, believing this to be the truth?

No! One can die for crimes of hate and destruction and misused power – not for beauty. Beauty is something for which to live!

Winds of Wisdom. What is beauty? Here it is an echo of all that is innate to man, an echo of his highest spiritual awareness. In reading this poem, it must be remembered that when man is referred to as a spiritual being, this means something he *is*, not something he *has*.

Magic, in this poem, is that extraordinary power and awareness of which mankind is capable.

The Mystery of Music again concerns music in the ancient and comprehensive sense. Like magic, it is the wisdom that is transcendental, which might seem to be unknown, and yet is known. Harmony and rhythm, in this poem, are allegorical and refer to the state of man when he is in complete agreement and understanding with himself, his family and friends, mankind, nature, the physical universe, and the universe of thought.

Vulcan's Mirror portrays another aspect of mirrors. Although the reflection produced by a mirror is an image of what is in front of it, it is not the thing itself. It is not even an exact replica of it, as right and left are reversed. Some mirrors are even made to distort the image. They contain enough truth to be recognizable, and yet can be very tricky and dangerous devices. They are capable of totally disorienting a

[1] *The Nine Muses: in Greek mythology, the nine goddesses who presided over all the arts: Calliope (epic poetry), Clio (history), Polyhymnia (religious music), Terpsichore (dance), Thalia (comedy), Melpomene (tragedy), Erato (lyric poetry), Euterpe (music), and Urania (astronomy).*

person and confusing his perceptions, to the point where he can become unable to distinguish between reality and illusion (the House of Mirrors in an amusement park is a good example).

Mirrors have been the subject of fables for a long time. *Alice Through the Looking Glass, Snow White,* and other fairy tales refer to magic mirrors. Jean Cocteau often used the idea of mirrors.

An image can be a counterpart: in *Mirrors for Identity,* nature is the counterpart of the soul of man – it is not the soul of man.

As long as the distinction between the image and the reality is maintained, there is no problem. However, it is the beginning of aberration and insanity when man begins to think that the image is the reality and that the actual reality does not exist. The result of this kind of thinking is a civilization that considers violence to be basic to the nature of man. A civilization that believes it is impossible to have a universe based on human understanding is based on the reverse image of what man knows to be true.

This is the image that Vulcan, the Roman god of fire, presents in his mirror of time.

Ave Phoenix (Hail Phoenix) is a reference to the fable of the Phoenix, a mythical bird, whose origin is given as Phoenician as well as Ethiopian. It was a bird of great beauty. Some say it lived for 500 years, others for up to 13,000 years. At the end of its life cycle, it was said to burn itself in fire and to rise from its own ashes, reborn, to live through another equally long cycle of years. It is a story that refers to immortality and represents mankind renewed after suffering.

In Silent Thunder refers to the rebirth which is awaited in *Primo Tempo.* In this last poem the philosophy which is based on man as a spiritual being, who is basically good, comes to life in our darkest moment.

It is the hope of modern man.

NOTES
SUR LES POEMES

Primo Tempo est le commencement. Tout le potentiel de l'homme, de la nature et de l'univers – son essence et non sa matière – attend une renaissance.

Miroirs Pour S'Identifier est basé sur certains concepts de la pensée dont le premier est relatif à la méditation, ou à la prise de conscience par l'homme de son identité spirituelle, de ses représentations, de ses sentiments et de ses idées, par rapport à la nature.

Le second est le reflet, ou l'image, rendu par le miroir, la contrepartie intangible du tangible. Ce sont des images, qui y sont liées, comme la pensée, mais qui demeurent abstraites.

Le troisième concept suit les lois de la physique. C'est l'action d'un corps qui change de direction après avoir heurté un autre corps; c'est le changement de direction des ondes lumineuses, sonores, solaires, etc. qui tombent sur une surface réflechissante. Par exemple, lorsque des ondes lumineuses viennent frapper la surface de séparation des deux milieux des ondes retournent en partie dans le premier milieu.[1]

Manus Terrae veut dire 'mains de la terre' en latin. Elle représente la source spirituelle de tout ce qui existe. Le thème en est semblable à celui de *Primo Tempo*.

Métamorphose concerne le changement complet de l'état d'être de l'homme. Le poème se réfère au concept le plus ancien qui est descendu de père en fils, de bouche à oreille, en musique et en paroles, c'est-à-dire : l'homme est une identité spirituelle. De nos jours, cette connaissance, à l'époque sacrée, est devenue profane. Les mots mêmes et les symboles ont changé et à présent, ils sont mal compris.

Par exemple, le dieu Pan. Le mot *pan* en ancien grec, veut dire *tout* (tel que dans

[1] *Les neuf Muses : en mythologie grec ; Calliope (poésie épique), Clio (l'histoire), Polyhymnia (musique religieuse), Terpsichore (la danse), Thalia (la comédie), Melpomène (la tragédie), Erato, (poésie lyrique), Euterpe (musique) et Urania (astronomie)*

le mot *pancromatique*, toutes les couleurs, ou *panorama*, une vue d'ensemble). Pan était le dieu de la nature et de la fertilité – un des dieux du Grand Tout. Il est représenté avec la tête, le thorax et les bras d'un homme et les pattes, les pieds et les cornes d'un bouc. Ce symbole de la vie fut transformé en diable, de couleur rouge ou noir, et en ajoutant une queue fourchue.

Le mot *démon* provient du grec *diamonion* qui veut dire de nature sacrée, par essence. De nos jours c'est un esprit malin.

Même le mot *esprit* a changé. Aujourd'hui il signifie un fantôme, une apparition, un spectre, ou tout autre phénomène qui fait peur la nuit.

Ces concepts font partie de toutes les choses qui étaient autrefois divines mais qui sont devenues profanes.

Dans *Métamorphose*, comme dans tous les poèmes, le mot *musique* est employé dans son sens pré-pythagoricien.

Pythagore fut à la fois philosophe, mathématicien, astronome et réformateur de la religion. Il inventa la gamme majeure en musique. Le mot *philosophe* n'était pas connu avant son temps, car il était inclus dans le mot *musique* qui voulait dire *l'art ou la science des Muses*.

Le mot *musique* était alors généralement utilisé pour les arts représentés par les neuf Muses[1] et comprenait le concept de la pensée, ou de l'âme, en tant que différenciée du corps. La mise en scène et l'interprétation musicale et vocale de la poésie lyrique n'étaient qu'une partie de *l'éducation musicale*. La musique comprenait la lecture, l'écriture, les sciences mathématiques et astronomiques, plus tous les arts littéraires. La musique fut appréciée à la fois dans son sens original et dans son sens général, mais aussi dans le sens moderne et restreint, surtout en tant qu'élément éducatif dans la formation du caractère, de la pensée, ou de l'âme.

Quand ce concept est étouffé ou devient désuet, il y a *métamorphose* de la pensée et de l'action de l'homme. Quelle est cette sagesse qui préconise la mort ou la souffrance au nom de la beauté? Et pourtant, combien de martyrs sont morts au nom de la bonté et de la 'vérité'? Combien de fois avons-nous entendu dire que 'l'art est né de la souffrance'? Combien d'artistes ont vécu et sont morts dans la misère, croyant que c'était la vérité?

Non! Il est, en effet, possible de mourir de ses crimes de haine, de destruction et de pouvoir abusé – mais non pour la beauté. Il faut vivre pour la beauté.

Vents de Sagesse. Qu'est-ce que la beauté? Ici, il s'agit d'un écho de tout ce qui est intrinsèque à l'homme, un écho de sa prise de conscience spirituelle, au niveau le plus élevé. A la lecture de ce poème, il faut se rappeler que lorsque l'on parle de l'homme en tant qu'identité spirituelle, il s'agit de ce qu'il *est* et non de ce qu'il possède.

La magie, dans ce poème, est ce pouvoir extraordinaire et cette connaissance dont l'homme est capable.

Le Mystère de la Musique concerne également la musique dans son sens général et ancien. Telle la magie, c'est la sagesse transcendantale qui pourrait paraître inconnue mais qui est, pourtant, connue. L'harmonie et le rythme, dans ce poème, sont allégoriques et se réfèrent à l'état de l'homme en accord total avec lui-même, avec sa famille et ses amis, avec l'humanité tout entière, avec la nature, l'univers physique et avec l'univers de la pensée.

Le Miroir de Vulcain dépeind un autre aspect des miroirs. Quoique le reflet du miroir soit l'image de ce qui se trouve devant lui, ce n'est pas la chose elle-même. Ce n'en est même pas une copie conforme puisque le côté droit et le côté gauche sont renversés.

Certains miroirs sont faits pour déformer les images; ils reflètent suffisamment de vérité pour qu'elles soient reconnues; toutefois, ils sont très mystifiants et dangereux. Ces miroirs sont capables de désorienter et de confondre les perceptions de l'homme, à un point tel que celui-ci devient incapable de distinguer la réalité de l'illusion (la Galerie des Miroirs dans un Lunapark, par exemple).

Les miroirs ont figuré dans des contes depuis très longtemps: *Alice au Pays des Merveilles*, *Blanche Neige* et d'autres contes de fées font allusion aux miroirs magiques. Jean Cocteau lui-même a souvent utilisé l'illusion des miroirs.

Une image est aussi un analogue: dans *Miroirs Pour S'Identifier*, la nature est la contrepartie de l'âme – ce n'est pas l'âme de l'homme lui-même. Tant que cette distinction est maintenue, il n'y a aucune problème.

Toutefois, l'erreur et la folie sont engendrées quand l'homme commence à croire que l'image devient la réalité et que la réalité n'existe pas. Par exemple, une civilisation qui considère la violence comme étant la nature fondamentale de l'homme est l'aboutissement de ce genre de pensée. Une civilisation qui croit impossible un univers basé sur la compréhension, est fondée sur l'image renversée de la vérité fondamentale de l'homme.

Voici donc l'image que présente Vulcain, le dieu romain du feu, dans son miroir du temps.

Ave Phoenix (je vous salue Phénix!) fait référence au mythe du phénix, cet oiseau légendaire dont l'origine est présumée phénicienne ou même éthiopienne. C'était un oiseau d'une rare beauté. Certains disent qu'il vécut 500 ans, d'autres 13.000 ans. A la fin de son cycle de vie, il s'immolait par le feu et surgissait des cendres, réincarné, pour revivre un cycle de vie tout aussi long. Cette histoire se réfère à l'immortalité et représente l'humanité renouvelée par la souffrance.

Tonnerre Sans Tambour se réfère à la renaissance qui est attendue dans *Primo Tempo*. Il s'agit de la philosophie selon laquelle l'homme est une identité spirituelle fondamentalement bonne, ce qui resurgit dans nos moments les plus sombres.

C'est le nouvel espoir de l'Homme.

REFERENCES

E. COBHAM BREWER, *Brewer's Dictionary of Phrase and Fable*, London, 1970.

Collins Latin–English, English–Latin Dictionary, London, 1974.

Encyclopaedia Britannica, London, 1961.

Encyclopaedia Britannica, *Standard Dictionary of the English Language* (International Edition), Chicago, 1960.

PIERRE GRIMAL, *Dictionnaire de la mythologie*, Paris, 1951.

Harrap's Standard French and English Dictionary (2 vols.), London, 1966.

L. RON HUBBARD, *Science of Survival*, Publications Organization, California & Copenhagen, 1970.

Larousse (3 vols.), Paris, 1975.

E. LITTRÉ, *Dictionnaire de la langue française*, Paris, 1863.

HENRY A. MURRAY, *Myth and Mythmaking*, New York, 1960.

The Random House Dictionary of the English Language (Unabridged), New York, 1970.

Music Lovers Encyclopedia.